Life from Within

Prayers by
Brother Roger of Taizé

Icons from the
Church of Reconciliation
in Taizé

GEOFFREY
CHAPMAN

MOWBRAY

The photographs

Front cover and facing prayer 8: Christ and Saint Menas, Coptic, 7th century, Louvre, Paris – facing prayers 1, 10, and 13: Icon of the Cross, by a brother of the Community, original in the Church of Reconciliation in Taizé (reproductions of this icon are taken from parish to parish and from country to country, as part of the 'pilgrimage of trust on earth') – facing prayers 2 and 12: The Resurrection of Christ, Russian, c. 1530 – facing prayers 3 and 14: The Trinity, Andrei Rublev, c. 1425, Tretyakov Gallery, Moscow – facing prayers 4 and 9: Icon of Mary, by a brother of the Community, Church of Reconciliation in Taizé – facing prayer 5: Baptism of Christ, by a brother of the Community, Church of Reconciliation in Taizé.

Published in Great Britain by
Geoffrey Chapman Mowbray
An imprint of Cassell Publishers Ltd
Villiers House, 41/47 Strand, London WC2N 5JE, England

Published in North America by **Westminster/John Knox Press**
100 Witherspoon Street, Kentucky 40202-1396, USA

Originally published 1988 as *Aus dem Innern leben*, © 1987 by Christophorus-Verlag GmbH, D-7800 Freiburg im Breisgau
English translation © 1990 Ateliers et Presses de Taizé,71250 Taizé Community, France

English-language edition first published 1990

ISBN 0-264-67214-3 (Geoffrey Chapman Mowbray)
      0-664-25162-5 (Westminster/John Knox Press)

Colour reproduction by H. & H. Schaufler, Freiburg im Breisgau
Typeset by Chapterhouse, The Cloisters, Formby, England
Printed and bound in Germany

Introduction

In Taizé, common prayer is at the heart of the meetings which week by week, summer and winter, bring together thousands of young people from every continent. As the bells ring out, the brothers and everyone else on the hill gather for prayer in the Church of Reconciliation three times a day.

Each midday, at the end of the silence which follows the Bible reading, Brother Roger, Taizé's founder, says a prayer which he has written that day. It is some of these prayers that have been chosen for this book. They give courage, in the midst of doubt and hesitation, to entrust ourselves to the living Christ. There, we can draw strength to go forward on the way of reconciliation; reconciliation among people, and with God.

After evening prayer, people stay on in church well into the night, singing or in silence. Some of them take this opportunity to share their concerns and their questioning with one of the brothers who remain in church to listen. Discreetly lit icons are like guides in the search to live from an inner life. The icons in this book are from the Church of Reconciliation in Taizé.

The fourteen prayers which make up the book can be used as short illustrated meditations, day by day, over two weeks.

1

Living God, you want us to have hearts
that are completely simple,
to the point that the complicated things in life
do not bring us to a halt.

Through the Holy Spirit,
the spirit of the Risen Christ,
you come to open up a way for us,
a way that is possible;
on it we understand that you love us first,
before we loved you.

2

O Risen Christ, you go down
to the lowest depths
of our human condition,
and you burden yourself
with what burdens us.
Still more, you even go
to visit those who have died
without being able to know you.

And even when within us
we can hear no refrain
of your presence,
you are there.
Through your Holy Spirit
you remain within us.

3

Lord Christ, if we had faith
that could move mountains,
yet without living charity,
what would we be?
You love us.
Without your Holy Spirit
who lives in our hearts,
what would we be?
You love us.
Taking everything on you,
you open for us a way towards faith,
towards trust in God,
who wants neither suffering
nor human distress.
Spirit of the Risen Christ,
Spirit of compassion,
Spirit of praise,
your love for each one of us
will never go away.

4

Seeking you, the Christ, is discovering
that you already loved us
and we did not know it.
Through the Gospel, you enable us
to catch a glimpse of how to love you,
right into our innermost solitude.
Happy those who surrender themselves to you.
Happy those who approach you
in trust of heart,
source of serene joy.

5

Holy Spirit, Spirit of the Living God,
you breathe in us
on all that is inadequate and fragile.

You make living water spring even
from our hurts themselves. And
through you, the valley of tears
becomes a place of wellsprings.

So, in an inner life
with neither beginning nor end,
your continual presence
makes new freshness break through.

6

Living God,
through your continuous presence in us,
you draw us out of ourselves and
our doubts. And you come to give our lives
a kind of shock of meaning.

You have confided to us, God's poor,
a mystery of hope. It sets within us an
inner light. In you, we find peace of heart
and unclouded joy
that touches the depth of the soul.

7

You were in me, Christ,
you were always there,
and I was not seeking you.
When I had found you, so often
I forgot you. But you continued
to love me. From the depths of my being,
a fire was rising to take hold of me.
I was burning for you to be everything
in my life. I was calling you:
You, the Christ, are the only way,
I have no other.

8

Although within us there are wounds,
Lord Christ, above all there is
the miracle of your mysterious presence.
Thus, made lighter or even set free,
we are going with you, the Christ,
from one discovery to another.

9

O God, we praise you
for the multitudes of women, men,
young people and children, who
are seeking to be witnesses of
peace, trust, and reconciliation
throughout the world.

In the footsteps of the holy witnesses
of all the ages, since Mary and the apostles,
to the believers of today,
grant us to prepare ourselves inwardly,
day after day, to place our trust
in the mystery of faith.

10

Lord Christ, you see us
sometimes strangers on the earth,
taken aback by the violence,
by the harshness of oppositions.

And you come to send out a gentle breeze
on the dry ground of our doubts,
and so prepare us to be bearers
of peace and of reconciliation.

11

Jesus, the Christ,
however little we know your Gospel,
it is light in our midst.
However little we grasp your presence,
it is light for us.

We search for you, Jesus, the Christ,
sometimes with uncertain steps,
but you have already come.
You bring light into our anxiousness.
You know
we would never want to choose darkness
but always welcome your inner light.

12

If you were not risen,
Lord Christ, to whom would we go
to discover a radiance
of the face of God?

If you were not risen,
we could not be together
to seek your communion.
We would not find in your presence
forgiveness,
wellspring of a new beginning.

If you were not risen,
where would we draw the energy
for following you
right to the end of our existence,
for choosing you again and anew?

13

O Christ, give us the gift
of looking towards you
at every moment.

So often we forget that you
live within us, that you are
praying within us,
that you are loving within us.

Your miracle in us is your trust
and your forgiveness, always offered
in that unique communion
which is called the Church.

14

Christ, Saviour of all life,
you come to us always.
Welcoming you in the peace of our nights,
in the silence of our days,
in the beauty of creation,
in the hours of great combat within,
welcoming you is knowing that you
will be with us in every situation,
always.

TAIZÉ

*– for preparing prayers, visits and meetings – for
private prayer and meditation – for groups and parishes –*

HIS LOVE IS A FIRE

Central writings with extracts from journals
Brother Roger of Taizé

THE TAIZÉ EXPERIENCE

A book of photographs by Vladimir Sichov
with text by Brother Roger

Both the above published in the USA by the Liturgical Press

**MEDITATIONS ON
THE WAY OF THE CROSS**
Mother Teresa of Calcutta and Brother Roger
of Taizé   (USA: Pilgrim Press)

**MARY MOTHER OF
RECONCILIATIONS**
Mother Teresa of Calcutta and Brother Roger
of Taizé   (USA: Paulist Press)

A PILGRIMAGE OF TRUST ON EARTH
Colour booklet with photographs and texts
about the community and the meetings in
Taizé

THE LETTER FROM TAIZÉ
Every two months, news from across the world,
themes for group reflection, texts for
meditation, prayers and daily Bible readings.

Subscriptions: write to Taizé, 71250 Taizé
Community, France

TAIZÉ – TRUST IS AT HAND
28 minute VHS PAL video-cassette
The community and the intercontinental
meetings, in Taizé, London, Madras, Paris,
UNESCO, etc.

PRAYING TOGETHER
in word and song   (USA: GIA)
Suggestions for prayer together, songs from
Taizé, and prayers by Brother Roger

CASSETTES
·**CANONS ET LITANIES – CANTATE –
ALLELUIA – RESURREXIT** (also on CD)
*Available in all main stores   (USA: GIA)
18 SONGS FROM TAIZÉ

THE STORY OF TAIZÉ
From Brother Roger's arrival in 1940, up to
the intercontinental meetings in summer 1987
J. L. González Balado

Geoffrey Chapman Mowbray
Stanley House, Fleets Lane, Poole BH15 3AJ, UK